SPORTS SUCCESS
Winning Women in Baseball and Softball

Marlene Targ Brill

BARRON'S

Photo credits:
Chapter One: FPG International
Chapters Three, Four, Six, and cover: Duomo Photography, Inc.
Chapter Five: Julie Croteau

Chapter Two line art by Bob Dorsey

All inquiries should be addressed to:
Barron's Educational Series, Inc.
250 Wireless Boulevard
Hauppauge, NY 11788
http://www.barronseduc.com

Library of Congress Catalog Card No.: 99-56984
International Standard Book No.: 0-7641-1231-7

Library of Congress Cataloging-in-Publication Data
Brill, Marlene Targ.
    Winning women in baseball and softball / by Marlene Targ Brill.
        p. cm — (Sport success)
    Includes bibliographical references (p.) and index.
    Summary: Surveys the history of women in baseball and softball,
how the games are played, what equipment is used, and the lives
of four famous players, Dot Richardson, Lisa Fernandez, Ila Borders,
and Julie Croteau.
    ISBN 0-7641-1231-7
    1. Women baseball players—United States—Juvenile literature
2. Women softball players—United States—Juvenile literature.
[1. Women baseball players. 2. Baseball players. 3. Women—
Biography.] I. Title.

GV880.7.B75 2000
796.357'082'092273—dc21
[B]   99-56984
                                             CIP

PRINTED IN THE UNITED STATES OF AMERICA
9 8 7 6 5 4 3 2 1

Contents

Acknowledgments

Many people helped me gather facts for this book. A special thank you goes to Dorothy (Dot) Richardson, USA Softball; Julie Croteau, Major League Baseball; Lisa Fernandez, USA Softball; Ila Borders, Madison Black Wolfs; Elsie Fernandez; Ray Croteau; Debbie Haley, St. Joseph High School; Erin Stibal, Lakewood Hall of Fame; Amy Symons, UCLA; Mike Stone, University of Massachusetts; Mike Zitz, Free Lance-Star and Fredericksburg Giants; Drew Russell, Women's National Fastpitch Association; Tom McCarthy, Progressive Sports Management; Brian McCall and Bill Plummer, Amateur Softball Association; John LaRue, Madison Black Wolves; Lorie Fenlason, Smith College; Sue Lukasik, American Women's Baseball Association; Sue Enquist, UCLA; Roger Murray, *Whittier Daily News*; Rolland Esslinger; Jim Wadley and Michael Bernier, Duluth-Superior Dukes; Nanci Young, Smith College Archives; Eddie Clinton, AAU; Charlie Phillips; Chris Diede, Vanguard University of Southern California; Tim Wiles, National Baseball Library; Gene Gumbs, Western New England College.

A Note to Readers

Once upon a time there were girls who loved to run, shoot baskets, speed skate, race bicycles and cars, and climb to great heights. These girls were different from active females today. Instead of being applauded for their talents, they were told they *couldn't* and *shouldn't* play most sports.

As recently as the late 1800s, adults offered a host of reasons why girls should stick to their dolls and needlework. One reason followed the belief that exercise hurt the frail female body and tired the mind. For example, some doctors assumed that riding caused "bicycle face," a scrunched-up look that supposedly came from the strain of sitting forward on a bicycle seat. Most likely, the tight corsets, high collars, long skirts, and big hats of the day led to the frowns.

Another common myth suggested that females who played like boys had something wrong with them. For one thing, active girls *looked* unladylike. Baron Pierre de Coubertin, founder of the modern Olympics, wrote in 1896: "It is indecent that spectators should be exposed to the risk of a woman being smashed before their very eyes."

Other critics assumed that females could never be as good in sports as males anyway. Therefore, they wondered, why would girls even bother to try? Such faultfinders called girls who played sports *tomboys* just because they wanted to have the same fun as boys.

Similar negative views of women in sports lingered into the 1960s. By then, females had started pushing for equal rights at home and at work. This led to Americans accepting that women and girls performed well in specific sports, such as gymnastics and figure skating.

Then the United States Congress passed the important Title IX law in 1972. Title IX ordered schools to give girls the same opportunities as boys to participate in sports. This meant that teams, equipment, and *all* sports had to be open to girls. Not long after the United States ruling, Canada and Australia passed similar laws. Each country required their schools to budget equal money for boys' and girls' sports. These laws championed the wild notion that girls would succeed if given the chance.

Little by little, schools began programming certain sports for girls. Some girls joined all-boy teams. Others battled to organize teams and leagues of their own. Gradually, females broke down barriers in sports such as sailboat racing, mountain climbing, wheelchair racing, coaching, and snowboarding that were mostly male-only arenas. Athletic girls who were once told to watch or cheerlead could now win their own medals.

At the same time girls entered more sports, new research replaced old-fashioned thinking that had kept girls on the sidelines. The Institute for Athletics and Education and the President's Council on Physical Fitness discovered that active girls earned better grades and were three times more likely to graduate from high school than their less active sisters. Girls who played sports were also more likely to go on to college and remain healthier as adults, developing fewer health problems, such as heart disease. In 1999, the Big Ten College Conference reported that a record 80 percent of women leaders in the top 500 U. S. companies participated in sports. These figures showed that girls who played sports felt better about themselves. They developed more confidence all-around because sports taught them what it means to be strong in body and mind.

Updated studies plus Title IX have had an amazing impact on girls participating in sports. In 1972, only 1 of every 27 girls joined high school varsity sports. Today, 1 in 3 girls participates, reflecting a positive trend in women's athletics. Now more girls play soccer than the number of girls who joined all sports in 1970. Consider, too, that in 1972 only 96 women athletes from the United States competed in the summer Olympics. By the summer of 1996, the roster had climbed to 280 women.

The 1996 and 1998 U.S. Women Olympic winners for soccer, baseball, basketball, and ice hockey—all new Olympic sports—were loaded with players who got their start on high school and college teams because of Title IX. These players confirm the success of 20 years of giving girls the opportunity to strut their sport's stuff. Now that's progress!

Still, we have a way to go toward equality for women in sports. One group to win over is the media. Except for sports such as ice skating, tennis, gymnastics, and now basketball, women athletes are invisible in most newspapers, television stations, and books. Donna Lopiano, former director of the Women's Sports Foundation, reported: "Until the 1990s, sports pages devoted more column inches to horses and dogs than to women's sports."

A 1996 study done at Vanderbilt University confirmed Ms. Lopiano's findings. After tracking national media, researchers found that women received only 7 to 11 percent of newspaper sports coverage. Television networks focused on skating, gymnastics, Olympic highlights, or special reports. Otherwise, women in sports were invisible to the media.

Little has changed going into the twenty-first century. The joys and talents of women athletes in many sports have gone unsung for too long. This book series seeks to broadcast the news that active girls and women are involved in all sports. So find the sport in the series that interests you most. Learn how other athletes have succeeded, often bucking great odds. Read how these talented women have fought battles so you can play any sport you choose. Then go out and play! Join the winning women and girls everywhere who are just warming up for a future of SPORT SUCCESS.

Marlene Targ Brill

Chapter One

On Your Mark, Get Set . . .

Baseball is the oldest team sport in the United States. Accounts of formal baseball games go back to before the Civil War (1861–65). These records show that baseball was played at least 45 years before the invention of basketball and 46 years before the first official football game.

Besides being an early sport, baseball has always been very popular. No other game has caught the imagination of so many Americans for so long. The nineteenth-century poet Walt Whitman once wrote: "It's our game... America's game. (It) has the snap, go, fling of the American atmosphere... (baseball) is just as important in the sum total of our historic life." And that historic life includes women's games, too.

Early Base Ball

Historians believe that American baseball evolved from various ball-and-stick games played in old England. During the 1700s, English players made one or more bases of stones, cloth, or stakes stuck into the ground. Rules for hitting the ball and distances between bases kept changing, and so did the names. Similar games with slightly different rules were called cricket, rounders, old-cat, barn ball, town ball, or base ball.

Author Jane Austen talked about baseball in her novel *Northanger Abbey*, which she began in 1803. In her story, Austen describes the character Catherine as someone who would "prefer cricket, baseball, riding on horseback, and running about the country at the age of fourteen, to books."

Organized Base Ball

Americans, male and female, have played ball-and-bat games since the late 1700s. According to legend, Abner Doubleday developed the current baseball game in 1839 while at school in Cooperstown, New York. Supposedly, Doubleday suggested a diamond-shaped field for the popular game of town ball. Then he threw bases on the diamond, giving baseball its name. Years later, an old homemade baseball thought to be Doubleday's was discovered on a farm near Cooperstown. To the National Baseball Hall of Fame, the ball proved Doubleday's connection to the game. In 1939, the organization built its museum in Cooperstown to celebrate the anniversary of Doubleday's baseball game.

The truth is there never was one creator of modern baseball. The sport developed over the years with many people contributing to today's rules. Daniel "Doc" Adams, president of the New York Base Ball Club in 1840, limited the game to nine innings. Before his time, a team had to score 21 runs to win, which often resulted in very long games.

In 1845, bank teller Alexander Cartwright formed the first organized team, the Knickerbocker Base Ball Club of New York City. Cartwright's main contribution to the game was to write down his rules, which set the standard for other teams. Cartwright's team played its opening game at Elysian Field in Hoboken, New Jersey, on June 19,1846. From then on, Americans everywhere caught baseball fever. As the Knickerbockers attracted fans around the country, reporters wrote of the "national pastime." By 1866, the *Chicago Tribune* announced that the nation was in the "Age of Baseball."

Ladies' Day

Women caught baseball fever, too. The game was fun. It was exciting. Girls who liked active outdoor games joined boys' teams. But as baseball became big business, women were left out of the action. The public disapproved of women playing any sport, much less one that could earn men some money. Pitcher and future sporting goods manufacturer Albert Spalding declared baseball "too strenuous for womankind." Most people agreed.

Many women gladly cheered from the stands. Club owners liked the idea of women at games. They believed that women calmed the rowdy fans. The *Ball Players Chronicle* claimed that women improved "the moral atmosphere of a base ball gathering,... (controlling) all outbursts of (wild) language which the excitement of a contest so frequently induces."

In 1867, the Knickerbockers declared the last Thursday of every month as Ladies' Day. On this day, the team charged less for females to attend, although a few women came other days, too. Club members were encouraged to bring wives, daughters, and girlfriends to cheer the team. To this day, many baseball teams offer special rates on certain days to attract female fans.

Girls' Clubs

During the late 1800s, some of the first female baseball teams came from women's colleges. Administrators listened to the few doctors who argued that sports contributed to a person's physical health and moral well-being. Vassar student Sophia Foster Richardson recalled that active play "puts her brain in fit condition for study."

Vassar, the first women's college, was founded in 1865. Within a year, Vassar students had formed two baseball clubs. Teams from different houses with names like the Resolutes and Laurel Base Ball Club competed on the open grass. Within ten years, Vassar students fielded eight baseball teams. Other women's schools followed Vassar's lead. Mostly, school clubs played against other teams from the same school. A few dared to compete with teams from other schools.

Athletes wore ankle-length skirts with the team name stitched on the belt, tight-collared long sleeve blouses, and high-button shoes. The heavy flowing layers ripped easily and slowed the runners. Fans gladly offered pins to keep players' skirts in ladylike form. But Minnie Stephens, Smith College class of

1883, wrote how a player's dress proved handy. "A vicious batter drove the ball directly into the belt line of her opponent, and had it not been for the rigid steel corset clasp worn in those days, she would have been knocked out completely."

Women in coed schools rarely enjoyed the same freedom to play baseball. In 1904, five women students at the University of Pennsylvania joined the men's baseball team. They played a few games before cheering crowds. Then university officials heard about the excitement. Within days, they banned women from playing baseball anywhere on school grounds.

In 1906, women at the Belfield Country Club near Philadelphia thrilled to play baseball despite head-to-toe clothing

Protests against women playing baseball grew louder, even at all-girls' schools. Parents considered team sports unwomanly because players competed as men did. Slowly, colleges eliminated their women's baseball teams. In 1923, the National Amateur Athletic Federation declared that women's college sports should be less competitive. School teams that were still going disbanded—at least for now.

Blondes, Brunettes, and Players in Corsets

After the first wave of college teams, the excitement of women's baseball spread beyond college campuses. In the beginning, most female teams were schemes devised by promoters to make money from the novelty of women playing in public. One such team was the Dolly Vardens of Philadelphia, the earliest recorded women's professional team. The name came from a fashion term for playful women in heavy makeup and corsets. The team was composed of African-American players who ran bases in red calico uniforms. Begun in 1867, the popular Dolly Vardens earned money for playing baseball two years before the first paid men's team, the Cincinnati Red Stockings.

Women's teams like the Dolly Vardens displayed better acting than athletic skills. Still, the public loved seeing women with little experience and heavy uniforms frolic around a baseball diamond. Clubs mushroomed around the country in the late 1800s, drawing large paying crowds.

From 1875 until the mid-1880s, three men operated a successful women's baseball club from Springfield, Illinois. They selected players based on hair color from 200 hopefuls and named two teams the Blondes and Brunettes. The women had little baseball experience. Their action-packed games contained lots of errors and high scores because many couldn't catch. Still, the women traveled from city to city playing their laughable form of baseball before adoring fans.

Several teams adopted the same names and game rules as the Blondes and Brunettes. On September 23, 1883, the *New York Times* reported how two teams with these names shocked 1,500 people at the Manhattan Athletic Club. "They played baseball in a very sad and sorrowful sort of way, as if the (whims) of the ball were too great for their struggling intellects." The reporter did allow that "four of the girls had become expert—for girls."

Bloomer Girls

In March 1871, the first professional league for men formed. The National Association for Professional Base Ball launched its opening season with ten teams, including the Cincinnati Red Stockings. The league became the forerunner of the National League of today.

Women took another twenty years to establish serious baseball teams. Between the 1890s and 1930s, women's teams called Bloomer Girls sprang up in most major cities around the nation. Bloomer Girls never

The First Woman Umpire

When Amanda Clement was seventeen, she went to watch her brother pitch in a semipro game in Hawarden, Iowa. The game before his, the umpire failed to show. Amanda's brother suggested that his sister make the calls. She called such a good game that she was asked to be umpire for her brother's game—for pay. The 1904 game was the first baseball game umpired by a woman for money. The game also launched a six-year career that paid for Amanda's college education.

played each other or formed a formal league. Instead, they traveled from town to town challenging men's amateur and semiprofessional teams. The adventurous women took their team name from Adelaide Jenks Bloomer. She was the women's rights pioneer who designed the loose-fitting pants many players wore.

Some Bloomer Girls were really men who joined the team to get valuable baseball training for breaking into professional baseball. Teenage boys and men proudly donned long skirts, and later bloomers, to catch or pitch. Male players were called "toppers" because of the curly wigs they wore to pass for females. Hall of Famers Joe Wood and Roger Hornsby received their baseball start as Bloomers.

Bloomer Girls played backbreaking schedules. In 1903, the Boston Bloomer Girls competed in 28 games in 26 days. They won every game. During one two-day weekend, the Bloomers recorded six wins in five different Oklahoma towns.

Softball: Women's Baseball

During the early 1900s, women everywhere joined local teams and clubs just for the chance to play ball. Many competed on women's or mixed teams. No matter how many times they took to the field, women ball players made news. Some received national attention for challenging accepted norms of the day. Unlike men, however, women had no organization to arrange games and tournaments. As a result, women's baseball all but disappeared during the 1920s, and many of the players' wonderful stories are lost today.

Meanwhile, physical education teachers searched for a way to make baseball less demanding on the female body. They thought that the newer game of softball could replace Bloomer Girl baseball. Softball's larger ball and smaller diamond slowed the game—the perfect substitute for baseball in school and recreation programs. The only problem was that game rules varied from place to place.

Modern softball actually began in 1887. According to experts, members of the Farragut Boat Club in Chicago invented the game with a boxing glove and broom handle instead of a ball and bat, but with rules similar to baseball. At first, the game went by names such as kitten ball, mush ball, women's baseball, and playground baseball, each with different rules. Some claimed that softball killed any hopes of women playing baseball. Others saw softball as a way for girls to continue playing a version of the game they loved.

Jackie Mitchell: Strikeout Queen

Joe Engle, owner of the Chattanooga Lookouts, thought Jackie Mitchell's arm was awesome—good enough to pitch for his team. So he hired the left-handed seventeen-year-old as a publicity stunt to boost attendance at an exhibition game with the New York Yankees on April 2, 1931. Jackie became the first woman to play men's professional baseball.

On the day of the game, Jackie discovered that her first batter was the great Babe Ruth. Unafraid, Jackie fired off four fastballs. One was called a ball, but the other three struck out the Babe. Next came Lou Gehrig, another powerhouse. One, two, three strikes, and he was out, too. Then Jackie walked Tony Lazzeri, and the manager sent in another pitcher. Jackie walked off the field to a standing ovation.

The game turned out to be Jackie's only chance to play in the big leagues. The baseball commissioner declared that a baseball life was "too strenuous" for a woman. Jackie still pitched on several semipro teams. But she always treasured the day when as a seventeen-year-old she struck out two baseball legends.

In 1933, the Amateur Softball Association (ASA) was formed to write one set of rules everyone could follow. The group's first job was to make the name *softball* official. One year later, the association printed a standard set of rules, creating a separate sport from baseball. Then the group hosted national tournaments for men *and* women.

Softball peaked in popularity during the 1940s. The country supported about 500,000 men's and women's teams, with one-third of the population attending games. Softball also became popular overseas. In 1952, the International Federation of Softball met to set standards for international play. The group worked to get softball recognized as an Olympic sport.

Many factories and businesses organized softball leagues to boost company spirit. One of the most famous company women's teams was the Raybestos Brakettes of Stratford, Connecticut. In 1965, the Brakettes took part in a world tour to spread women's softball. The same year, the team played in the first Women's Fast-Pitch tournament in Melbourne, Australia. Between 1942 and 1973, the Brakettes won 25 Women's Fast-Pitch national titles. Their successes in these and other tournaments helped develop the sport in the United States and around the world.

All-American Girls Professional Baseball League

In 1941, the United States entered World War II, and most professional baseball players went to fight. Chewing-gum king and Chicago Cubs owner, Philip Wrigley, worried that professional baseball might end without its stars. He decided to form a women's league to fill major league stadiums.

In 1943, the All-American Girls Professional Baseball League (AAGPBL) launched its opening season with four teams—the Rockford Peaches, South

First Woman Big Leaguer

An unwritten law barred blacks from playing professional baseball. Negro leagues developed to fill the gap for talented black men, but black women had no teams. In 1953, the league's Indianapolis Clowns hired Marcenia "Toni" Stone for the season. Toni became the first woman on a major-league team and the first to play in a men's uniform—not a skirt or shorts.

Mostly, Toni played exhibition games or only a few innings a game during the season. But she made her limited game-time count. On Easter Sunday in 1953, Toni was the only batter to hit off the famous pitcher Satchel Paige in an Omaha, Nebraska, standoff. The next year, she was traded to the Monarchs and replaced by two more women. After one season with the Monarchs, Toni returned to the minor leagues, still playing with men.

Bend Blue Sox, Racine Belles, and Kenosha Comets. Within a few years, the women's league expanded to ten teams. For the first time, women's baseball received the widespread funding and public support it deserved.

At first, the women played a game more like softball than baseball. Gradually, the league introduced overhand pitching, a smaller ball, greater distances between bases, and stealing bases. Fans loved the changes. They thrilled at seeing skilled players like Peaches first base-woman Dottie Kamenshek catch a ball while doing splits. They followed closely in 1946 as Belles Sophie Kurys stole 201 bases, a professional record for any league that still stands. Blue Sox shortstop Dottie Schroeder told an author: "Once they (fans) saw how well we played ball, they were hooked." Reporters dubbed the athletes "Belles of the Ball Game."

Wrigley insisted on a polite, ladylike image for his players. Players were forbidden to drink, gamble, wear slacks in public, stay out too late, or date without permission. For two seasons, Wrigley required them to attend charm school. Here they learned to apply makeup, fix their hair, and brush up on "social graces," such as talking with fans. A $10 fine awaited anyone removed from a game. But looking messy in public cost a stiffer fine of $50.

During games, players wore short-skirted uniforms with elastic undershorts and socks rolled below the knee. Skirts got in the way of windmill wind-ups for underhand pitching. And they offered little protection. In *Women in Baseball,* Helen Callagan remembered: "We'd have strawberries (scrapes) on our legs from sliding in skirts,... and the chaperones would just tape us up, and out we'd go."

Baseball Blues

The AAGPBL lasted for nine years—until 1954. During that time, almost 500 women earned their living playing professional baseball before millions of people. Despite the interest created by the AAGPBL, only a handful of women's baseball leagues have developed since. Few have lasted very long. Many big cities are home to amateur leagues. But they continue more as labors of love for small groups of players, their families, and friends.

Sue Lukasik belongs to one such group that started in 1988. The American Women's Baseball Association, a recreational league near Chicago, once sported four teams with a ten-game season. Now they can barely fill one team. "After the furor of *A League of Their Own* ended, we had a hard time finding players," Sue explained. "Then the sponsors dried up. We had a hard time finding tournament fields when men were playing. So we were forced to limit our games."

Some women have played either against or on men's teams. In 1993, the Coors Brewing Company held tryouts for an all-female baseball team, the Silver Bullets of Colorado. At first, the Bullets played in a men's professional league, which gained the team lots of attention. But they lost their first game 19–0. Coaches decided that the women should compete against men's college and semipro teams instead. The Bullets still ended their first season with only 6 wins out of 36 games. By 1997, however, they had won 23 games and lost 22. But Coors pulled out anyway, leaving the Bullets without backing and the players without a team.

Softball Fills In

Professional women's softball leagues have come and gone, too. Softball legend Joan Joyce and tennis star Billie Jean King founded the first women's softball league in 1976. The International Women's Professional

Softball Association, featuring ten teams from cities across the nation, lasted only four seasons before lack of money and playing fields caused it to die.

In 1997, the Women's Pro Softball League burst onto the sports scene. Fans of six teams in the eastern United States packed stadiums to watch the world's top fast-pitch players. If backing and full houses continue, the league plans to add teams from regions further west.

Softball holds the greater promise for girls who care to play as adults. Although few girls have the chance to play high school and college baseball, most schools encourage girls' softball. More than 10 million women and girls play in recreational leagues nationwide, and worldwide softball is played in almost 80 countries. The ASA sends top players to represent the United States in annual international competitions. The women's national team has stolen every major world championship, bringing home the gold in the last four Pan-American Games alone.

Turning a New Century

Of all the international competitions, the 1996 Olympics provided the biggest boost for women's softball. In their first women's softball Olympics, the U.S. softball team overpowered strong teams from China and Australia. When the United States won the gold medal, they did more than win another contest, however. Talented Olympic players showed girls every-

Little League for Boys and Girls

In 1939, Carl Stotz began Little League baseball in Williamsport, Pennsylvania. Stotz wanted his young nephews to play organized baseball with uniforms, equipment, and a season of games. By the league's fiftieth birthday, the original boys' teams had expanded to 2.5 million six-to eighteen-year-olds in more than 7,000 leagues in 33 nations.

Until 1974, Little League barred girls from playing organized baseball. The girl credited with changing the no-girl policy was Maria Pepe of Hoboken, New Jersey. In 1972, Maria made the Hoboken Young Democrats Little League team. But officers at national Little League headquarters objected to girls on teams. They threatened to expel Hoboken from the league if Maria played.

Maria left the team. But the National Organization for Women filed a lawsuit on her behalf. A long drawn-out court battle followed. Communities split over whether to allow girls into baseball leagues. Similar lawsuits appeared in other states. After two years, the judge ruled that it was illegal to prevent any child from joining a team because she was a girl.

Little League tried to sidestep the order by creating a girls' softball league. Some girls refused to be tricked. Maria had turned thirteen, too old for her team. However, many other brave girls stepped forward to become the first females on their Little League teams.

where that from now on they have somewhere to go with their skills beyond college.

The popularity of softball does not mean that girls never play baseball. Indeed, girls' baseball is growing, whereas softball numbers are shrinking. According to a 1998 National Sporting Goods Association study, girls from seven to seventeen played 29 percent more baseball and 6 percent less softball than they did in the previous five years. Many break barriers on boys' and men's teams. Others keep trying to form lasting leagues of their own.

But too many roadblocks still exist. For example, Los Angeles boys play on perfect grassy fields, while their ball-playing sisters shovel dirt to fill in dangerous potholes in fields they are given. Still, change is in the air. Girls with a desire to overcome barriers can dream of playing whichever sport they love. They know about women from history who have played either game. Today, they see winning women who achieve sport success in both baseball and softball.

Chapter Two

How to Play

Baseball and softball look simple to play. Yet, they offer great challenges. Players often change the course of a game with one smash hit or a leap for a surprise catch. According to poet Marianne Moore: "Baseball is like writing. You can never tell with either how it will go or what you will do; generating excitement—a fever in the victim—pitcher, catcher, fielder, batter."

Play Ball

Baseball and softball are games played by two teams on a large field. The object of these games is to see which of the two teams scores the most points, or runs. To get a run, the batting team, or offense, chooses one player at a time to hit the ball with a bat. After the bat connects with a ball, the *batter* tries to score by running around four bases on a field. Meanwhile, the pitching team, or defense, uses its players on the field to catch the ball and tag the runner before she reaches a base.

If a runner gets tagged, she is out. A batter who swings three times without hitting the ball is also out. Once each team has a chance for three outs, a new inning begins. Every game lasts for nine *innings*. If the score is tied after nine innings, the game continues for extra innings until one team breaks the tie.

Diamonds Are a Girl's Best Friend

The baseball field is called a *diamond* because of its shape. Four *bases*—one on each diamond point—form the diamond. *Home plate* is the starting and ending point at the lower corner. First base is the right corner, second base lies at the top point, and third base is the corner to the left of home plate. The pitcher's mound sits in the middle of the diamond.

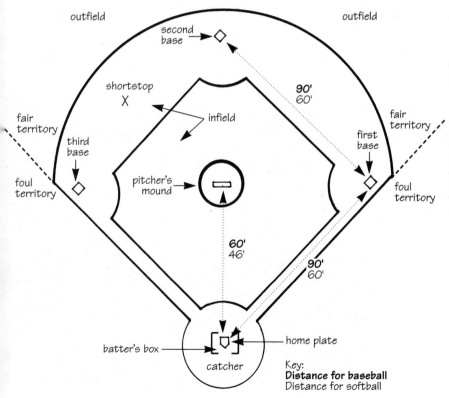

Baseball and softball fields have the same design.

To score a run, a batter must race counterclockwise from home plate to each base and home again. The distance between each base depends upon who is playing and the size of the diamond. Professional teams play on diamonds with bases 90 feet (27 meters) apart and 60 feet, 6 inches (18.2 meters) between the pitcher's mound and home plate. Younger or unpaid athletes usually play on fields with 60 feet (18 meters) between bases and 46 feet (14 meters) from home plate to the pitcher.

Everything inside the diamond is called the *infield*. The *outfield* extends away from home plate, beyond the diamond. The area outside the diamond lines is called *fair territory* and is part of the playing field.

The lines that reach out from home plate mark *foul territory*. Any ball hit into foul territory is a *foul ball* and considered out-of-bounds. That includes the area from home plate to the nearest fence behind the diamond, which must extend 250 feet (76 meters) or more.

Batter Up

Players on the two teams take turns batting, or trying to score. Each team manager creates a list that shows the *batting order*. One after another, the batters step into the *batter's box* next to home base, or home plate, to hit the ball. As a ball whizzes in, several things may happen:

- The batter swings at the ball and misses. This results in a *strike* call. Batters who receive three strikes are out. Then the next batter from the team's list enters the batter's box.

- The batter never swings, but the ball comes within the *strike zone*. This is an imaginary space where the ball should be pitched so the batter can reasonably hit it. The exact strike zone depends on how the batter stands. Usually, the strike zone parallels the area between the batter's mid-chest and top of the knees. Balls that pass through this area without being hit are strikes.
- The ball shoots outside the strike zone, and the batter never swings. Then a *ball* is called. After four balls, the batter is allowed to *walk*, or advance to first base.
- The batter swings at the incoming ball and connects. If the ball goes into foul territory, it counts as a strike. Two foul balls equal two strikes. After that, foul balls do not count against the batter.

If the ball goes into fair territory, it is a *hit*. Then the batter becomes a *runner*, charging toward first base. The batter who reaches first base before the ball is called *safe*. Should the next batter get a walk or hit, the one on first base runs to second base.

Sometimes, hits soar so far that the batter has

time to reach more than one base at a time. The bat-ter-runner who safely reaches the second base gets a *double play*. If she makes it to third base, she earns a *triple play*. A batter who hits a ball that allows her to circle all the bases scores a *home run*. Any players who are on base when a batter hits a home run can run home and score, too. Runners can also *steal* a base by continuing to the next base without a batter's hit or walk.

One or more *umpires* are the game officials who decide whether a runner is safe or out. Usually, an umpire stands behind the catcher. This spot allows the umpire to judge whether a pitch is a strike or a ball. Whatever an umpire decides is the final word.

The Defending Team

The pitching, or defending, team sends nine players onto the field. Each has a special position there.

Pitcher. Plays begin when the pitcher throws, or pitches, the ball. A pitcher's job is to make the opposing batter miss the ball or hit it where a team-mate can easily catch it. Good pitchers throw a mix of fast balls, slower balls, and curve balls to trick the batter. They must have a strong arm and good aim to throw the ball within the strike zone.

Catcher. The catcher crouches behind home plate to catch whatever balls the batter doesn't hit. Catchers need to throw far enough to reach where a runner is trying to steal a base. They must also help the pitcher decide how to throw the ball.

Infielders. The first, second, and third base players and shortstop play infield. These players try to catch hits and touch a base before the runner. Many times, they catch the ball and *tag* the runner out by touching the person with the ball. Infielders must be sharp, quick, and willing to stretch and dive for balls.

Outfielders. Three outfielders defend right field, center field, and left field. These players must be fast runners to cover the large outfield and sharp throwers to quickly get the ball where it needs to go to put a runner out.

Equipment

For the first Little League game in 1939, equipment was cheap and mostly homemade. A catcher's mask cost $1.67 and uniforms $1.58. Mothers sewed lettering on the uniforms. They stuffed wood shavings into cheap duck cloth to shape bases. Add the bat and a ball, and the players were ready to play baseball.

Today, costs are higher, and most equipment is factory-made. Modern baseball and softball leagues also tend to worry more about safety, so some players wear more padding. But the basic equipment needs are the same for either game—a ball, a bat, a glove, four bases, and, if the team is lucky, a uniform

The Ball. According to official rules, a baseball must be between 9 and $9^1/4$ inches (22.9 to 23 centimeters) in circumference, the distance around the outside of the ball. It can never weigh less than 5 ounces (140 grams) or more than $5^1/4$ ounces (149 grams). Balls are made of yarn wound tightly around a small cork or rubber center. Two strips of horsehide or cowhide are stitched together over the yarn. Balls for children's leagues are the same size, but they can be made of different materials.

The Amateur Softball Association (ASA) requires that softballs be between $11^7/8$ and $12^1/8$ inches (30.2 to 30.8 centimeters) around. They must weigh between $6^1/4$ and 7 ounces (183 to 200 grams). In this game, the size decreases as players age.

The Bat. Bats are rounded sticks made from a solid piece of wood or metal. Their weight can vary, and they can extend up to 42 inches (106.7 centimeters) in length. But bats can measure no more than $2^3/4$ inches (7 centimeters) wide at the fattest point. Although youth leagues use both wood and aluminum bats, professional ball players hit only with wooden bats.

Gloves. Catchers use a heavily padded glove called a *mitt*. The thumb fits into one section, and the other fingers each go into different sections. Mitts can never be more than 38 inches (96.5 centimeters) around and $15^1/2$ inches (39 centimeters) from top to bottom. Other defensive players wear smaller gloves that are less than 12 inches (30.5 centimeters) long and $7^3/4$ inches (19.7 centimeters) wide.

Uniforms. Players on a team wear uniforms that have the same style and color. They dress in pants that protect legs from sliding and shirts that show a number on the back to identify each player. Those who play in dirt or grassy fields find they run better with cleats, or shoes with rounded spikes on the bottom, on their feet. Spikes can be plastic or metal, but most youth games prohibit metal cleats. Many leagues now require helmets to protect batters from wayward pitches. Players often wear caps to block the sun when on the open field.

The catcher is the only player who needs special equipment. Besides a helmet and a mitt, catchers wear a face mask, a chest protector, and shin guards to shield the body.

How Is Softball Different?

Softball and baseball rules and methods are similar. The same number of people on a team try to reach the same goal—to score the most runs and win. Still, those who play either sport believe that each is a totally different game.

Softball games last only seven innings. They are played with balls that are larger than baseballs and softer, which gives softball its name and makes for slower pitches and shorter hits.

Softball diamonds are smaller than baseball diamonds. The distance between softball bases is 60 feet (18 meters), instead of 90 feet (27 meters). Pitchers throw 46 feet (14 meters) from the mound to home plate, 14 feet (4.2 meters) less than in baseball. With some forms of softball, players cannot steal bases. In

27

others, as long as the ball has left the pitcher's hands, a player can bolt to the next base.

The biggest difference between baseball and softball is pitching style. In baseball, pitchers throw overhand. Softball calls for underhand pitching only. Leagues' rules vary, however, depending upon what type of underhand throw the pitcher uses.

Fast-pitch softball involves a pitch delivered in a straight line. Pitchers wind up their arm like a windmill before letting the ball go. This method increases the speed of the ball, sometimes up to 90 miles an

Pitchers throw overhand for baseball.

Both fast- and slow-pitch softball require underhand throws.

hour. The speed and strength of the pitch, called a windmill pitch, come closer to pitching in baseball than to pitching in *slow-pitch* softball. A legal slow-pitch throw travels in an arc. The arc must be at least 3 feet (0.9 meters) but not more than 10 feet (3 meters) above the ground before reaching the plate.

Although there are few differences between softball and baseball, each sport has its own following of eager players. As long as the two games continue, there will always be girls and women who play baseball and softball. Here are some of their stories.

Chapter Three

Dorothy "Dot" Richardson

orothy "Dot" Richardson knew many doors were closed to her because she was a girl. Still, she kept dreaming—of making a ball team, of becoming a surgeon. She never gave up hope. With time and lots of practice, her dreams began to come true. At age thirteen, she became the youngest player in history to join a women's semipro softball team. She knocked down school barriers by receiving sports honors never accorded a girl. Then she made medical school while playing softball. Her biggest triumph, however, came during the 1996 Olympics, while on leave from surgery training. That's when "Doctor Shortstop" delivered the championship-winning hit that gave the United States the gold.

On the Move

Dorothy was born on September 22, 1961, to Joyce and Kenneth Richardson. Young Dorothy, the fourth of five children, was a mover. She often drove her parents crazy by being so active. "I had a difficult time sitting and watching TV," Dorothy said. "I always felt coordinated and loved challenges, so I got into more. I'd climb cabinets and trees and fall down stairs. My parents had to put a 9-foot-high fence in our yard, so I wouldn't climb out."

Dorothy's family was on the move, too. Her father was an Air Force officer, which meant that the family changed hometowns often. After she was born, Dot, her parents, her older brother Kenny, and her two older sisters Kathy and Laurie went to Guam. A year later, brother Lonnie was born, and the family relocated again. With each new setting, Dorothy discovered another sport. When Dorothy turned ten, her father retired, and the family settled in Orlando, Florida.

Standout in Sports

By second grade, Dot's mother knew her daughter had a gift for athletics. Dot could outrun, outshoot, and outkick boys who were three years older. Of all the sports, Dorothy liked baseball the most. At age six, she dreamed of receiving an Olympic gold medal for baseball.

> *"I often asked why I was given talent and enjoyment in a world with so few opportunities. I could accept any reason, but... because you're a girl."*

Dorothy's brothers both played Little League, and her father coached. Dorothy asked to join a team, too. But Little League rules prohibited girls on teams back then. Each time she applied for a team, she was rejected.

"I often asked why I was given talent and enjoyment in a world with so few opportunities," Dot said. "I could accept any reason, but . . . because you're a girl."

Dorothy's family tried to encourage her interests. Her brothers played catch with her. Her father made her bat girl for Lonnie and Kenny's team. That way, she practiced with the boys. But Dorothy's belief in herself and her talents came from something her mother said.

"When I asked my mom why I can't play Little League, she said because I would strike out all the boys, and parents would have trouble with it," Dot remembered. "That answer supported me, rather than saying I couldn't play."

A Breakthrough

During sixth grade, Dot experienced her first taste of an organized team, but not the one she expected. A Little League coach watched Dot pitch to her brothers before a game. He liked her pitching arm enough to ask her to join his team. Dot jumped at the chance. Then the coach told her to cut her hair short and answer to the name Bob.

"Even though that was something I wanted more than anything," she remembered, "I thanked him and said I wouldn't feel right if I had to hide who I was."

Dot felt let down—but not for long. Soon another man appeared and asked her to talk with a coach he knew. To Dot's surprise, the coach was a woman.

The coach asked Dot if she had ever played softball. Then she told her to get on third base and take some ground balls. After a few throws, the coach asked Dot her age and whether she'd like to join her team.

Before that day, Dot had never heard of softball, let alone the Union Park Jets. Most women on the Jets were in their twenties. They played on the Amateur Softball Association women's Class A fast-pitch team that traveled within a couple-state region. The coach's jaw dropped when she heard that Dot was only ten.

Welcome to Softball

Dorothy was thrilled when her parents agreed to let her play. Finally, she had a team, complete with red, white, and blue uniforms. She went from no team-mates to starting at third base and hitting first in the lineup. The girl who had never played softball hit off 50- to 60-mph pitches.

From the first game, Dot knew softball was her sport. By the end of the season, she had made the league's all-star team. Just before the tournament in Tennessee, however, Dot cut her foot badly. She was heartbroken to miss the games. But being home enabled her to register for the highest level fast-pitch softball camp for the Orlando Rebels.

Just two weeks after the injury, Dot limped into Varner Stadium in Orlando. At tryouts, the eager, freckle-faced eleven-year-old hobbled around the bases. Dot's throwing impressed Coach Marge Ricker.

She allowed Dot to stay at the league camp even though the cutoff age was fourteen. At the end of camp, Ricker offered Dot one of two spots as bat girl. Dot couldn't play in games, and she had to lug bats. But she went to practices three evenings a week and to games, which meant she could study the skills of top players.

During the sixth inning of the second game of a double-header, Orlando was beating Alabama 10–0. The coach surprised Dot by putting her into the game in right field. When it was her turn to bat, she got a base hit, which scored a run. Then she stole second base and was hit in to score a run. In right field again, Dot fielded a fly ball and threw a batter out at first, ending the game.

"Everything good that could happen to a player happened to me that night," Dot wrote in *Living the Dream.* "We had won and I had played in the major leagues!"

The next season (1975), Dot attended camp again. After this camp, Ricker offered Dot a place with the Rebels. The association had dropped the age rule. At thirteen years, Dot became the youngest person, girl or boy, to ever play in the ASA Major Leagues.

On the Road

Ricker taught Dot to bat left-handed because of her speed. She wanted to make sure that Dot never formed bad habits hitting right-handed for school and church leagues. Coaches marveled at how easily Dot shifted between slow- and fast-pitch softball.

Dot loved traveling to games in a motor home with the Orlando Rebels. Even though being on the team was like having 15 mothers, Dot felt very grown up. She received $5 a day for meal money, a lot of money back then for a thirteen-year-old to buy whatever she wanted.

"I once drank a chocolate milkshake for every meal on a three-week tour," Dot admitted. "I came home with pimples on my chest. I haven't had a chocolate milkshake since."

Ricker put Dot first in the batting lineup and in right field for defense. Later, Ricker switched Dot to shortstop. People were amazed that a thirteen-year-old could hold her own in the majors. Fans cheered her throws. Little girls wanted her autograph. Reporters swarmed Dot after each game. Often, they asked whether being so young affected her game.

"It does not really matter how old you are," Dot wrote, "it matters how well you play."

Back at School

Meanwhile, Dot was making her mark at Union Park Junior High School. Her grades were good, especially in math, and she loved to draw and sing. Not surprisingly, Dot's favorite class was physical education.

Most people considered her a tomboy. She received her share of insults for running faster or playing better than the boys. In seventh grade, Dot tried to fit in by trying out for cheerleading. "Thank goodness, I didn't make it," Dot wrote. "Because if I had made it, I wouldn't have been able to compete in the four sports I chose to play."

After that disaster, Dot just tried not paying attention to what others said. It paid off. At graduation, she received most valuable player awards for all four sports she played—volleyball, basketball, softball, and track. The greatest honor came when the principal handed her the school's Outstanding Athlete Award. She was the first girl at Union Park to receive the plaque.

"I was judged by my performance instead of my gender or race," Dot beamed.

Dot continued her successes at Colonial High School. Her grades remained high all three years, and

> **"I was judged by my performance instead of my gender or race."**

she made All-Conference in every sport she played. Dot's freshman year, she made the top tennis, volleyball, basketball, and slow-pitch softball teams. By her senior year, she had dropped tennis and added track.

"The reason I didn't participate (in track) was because I ... was afraid of being beaten. I grew up during those two years. I learned the importance of facing the challenge."

37

During her last year, Dot broke new ground at Colonial. Each year, coaches chose one senior as Outstanding Athlete of the Year. That person had always been a boy. The problem was Dot's standings were unmatched. Coaches were forced to seriously consider her for the award. As a compromise, they gave both Dot and a boy the award.

Hope for the Olympics

In 1979, the Olympic Committee announced that women's softball would be part of the Pan-American Games. USA Softball coach Ralph Raymond had seen Dot play a Rebels game, and made sure she was invited to USA team tryouts. The night Dot graduated from high school, she boarded a plane for the Olympic Training Center in Colorado Springs. The next day, she was assigned to second base.

Dot played her heart out in tryout games for the next week. USA Softball rewarded her hard work. At age seventeen, Dot became the youngest starter chosen for the U.S. Pan-American team. Standing 5 feet, 4 inches, Dot was one of the smallest athletes on the team. Therefore, she received one of the smallest uniforms, including a jersey with the number one on the back.

"When I wear the number one, it is with pride for the United States," Dot said, delighted.

On to College

Before high school graduation, Dot received many college scholarship offers for basketball, volleyball, and softball—both slow-pitch and fast-pitch. The only schools Dot took seriously supported strong fast-pitch softball teams.

Although Dot preferred to go to school in California, when Western Illinois University in Macomb offered her a full scholarship to play fast-pitch, she took it.

The fall of 1979, Dot began courses in athletic training and health. She discovered that she loved the health courses. Her second semester, she volunteered with the school physical therapist. These experiences sparked an interest in becoming a doctor.

On the field, Dot had a great year. She played basketball and, for the first time, field hockey. But playing shortstop again in softball brought the most rewards. "I led the country with a .480 batting average and was nominated for the Broderick Award for the best female softball athlete," Dot said. "Cool for a freshman."

Time for Change

The end of her first year in college, Dot received an offer to play softball at the University of California in Los Angeles (UCLA), the school that had won every major championship title. Dot was torn. She worried about disappointing her Western coach and team.

"Then my big sister Kathy called," Dot remembered. "She said 'You should go. You always wanted to go.' I decided to switch to UCLA and compete in the school of my dreams."

Three years (1981–1983) at UCLA proved a great choice. The Bruins went to national championships each year. Dot earned three All-American titles and led the Bruins in hitting. Years later, the NCAA named her Player of the Decade.

"Dot did a tremendous job of leading our team," said Sue Enquist, UCLA coach. "She had a great range of coverage from second to third base. She had a great arm. Offensively, she was our lead-off batter, which is a critical and pressure-filled position."

Dot gained a reputation for being unbeatable. Other coaches often told their pitchers to walk her. That way, she couldn't do too much damage, like hit a home run. Even if she was walked, her love of the game boosted the level of play for her teammates."

"Dot came to the park every day with a level of passion about the game that was unmatched," Sue added. "The second game of the 1983 national championships stands out as an example. Eight of our nine starters got food poisoning. Dottie was probably sickest. I remember her hitting a ball into outfield, stretching a single into a double, and vomiting on second base. She would not come out of the game. When you see someone with that kind of courage, it raises the entire team's game."

Mixing Medical School and Two Softball Teams

In 1984, Dot graduated from UCLA with a degree in the study of movement. That same year, Olympic coach Raymond asked Dot if she would like to play shortstop for his Raybestos Brakettes. Dot felt honored. The Brakettes were among the top ASA teams.

Dot went home after graduation unsure about becoming a doctor. She began and completed a master's program in health at Adelphi University in New York. The university gave her free housing and allowed her to coach.

"That's when I learned how to teach," Dot said. "This inspired me to help others learn more about the sport and improve their skills." Dot made her first videotapes about hitting and fielding.

By the time she left Adelphi, Dot had resolved to try medical school. In 1989, she enrolled in the University of Louisville. She thought she should retire from softball, but her school schedule allowed her weekends off and one free summer month. The juggling act began.

After a week of classes, Dot often made a mad dash to the airport. She traveled cross-country to a waiting car at the other end. Many days, she changed from her white doctor coat into a Brakettes uniform in the car. During her month off, she played for the U.S. team.

At times, Dot's study schedule required that she miss games and tournaments. For the most part, she felt that the juggling act worked. Grades were good, and she continued to rack up softball honors. She became a 16-time ASA All-American, 7-time winner of the Erv Lind Award for the best defense in national fast-pitch championships, and a major reason the United States earned a host of gold medals in international competitions.

Difficult Road to the Olympics

Then Dot hit her first snag. At the end of each two years, medical students took state boards. Dot had sailed through her first year and expected to pass the next year. But she failed the second-year exam. Rather than take the test over, she chose to retake her second year of classes.

"I felt I had focused too much on athletics," Dot said. "After that letdown, I devoted myself to my classes. The next year I passed. It was a lesson of balance."

But the scales had tipped in favor of school. After the exam, Dot flew to tryouts for the USA Pan-American team. It had been nine months since she touched a ball. She performed poorly during the week-long tryouts. Yet, she assumed she would make the team based on her past record. She was wrong. For the first time, the coaches left Dot off the national team.

Dot lunges for a ball at the 1996 Olympics.

Dot's last year of medical school went more smoothly. She passed her boards and graduated. That was 1993, the same year she heard that softball would be an official sport at the 1996 Olympics. Not long after, Dot returned to UCLA, this time for further study to become an orthopedic surgeon (a doctor who treats bones and muscles). She said little about her Olympic dreams at school, not knowing whether she could even find time to study and compete. In the end, Dot decided to go for both. She determined to truly balance school, softball, and the enormous number of speaking dates and kids' programs that accompanied her growing fame.

Coach Raymond announced that he was retiring from the Brakettes. That left Dot free to switch to the California Commotion, which helped control weekend travel. To keep in shape, she bought a treadmill, weights, and a batting tree and net. She lifted weights two to three times a week and jogged and swung at balls whenever time allowed.

Dreams Fulfilled

In 1995, after Dot's second year in the surgery program, her boss gave her a year off for Olympic training. On July 1, the lively 5-foot, 4 1/2-inch shortstop arrived in Denver, Colorado, for the Olympic Festival. Top athletes competed here for the chance to represent the United States at the 1996 Olympics. To Dot's surprise, she was chosen to carry the festival torch for all athletes.

"It was breathtaking," Dot enthusiastically told the *Orlando Sentinel.* "I felt so proud representing all those athletes."

The next day Dot played in the first exhibition game. During the game, she swung wide and twisted her neck. She tried resting, playing, and sitting out for a day. Nothing made her feel better. Then came the final tryout game. She knew she had to play or give up her dream. Still hurting, Dot smacked a home run out to center field, clinching a spot on the Olympic team.

For Dot, the Olympics were a dream come true. She hit the first Olympic home run during the first game with Puerto Rico, which the United States won 10–0. During the next game, Dot hit a home run that helped the United States win 9–0. In the eighth and final game with China, she hit another homer, this time bringing in two runs and clinching the game to win 3–1 and the gold. Dot finished the Olympics with an amazing three home runs and seven runs batted in.

But her proudest moment came on the riser as she accepted her gold medal. "The 1996 Olympics was more than the highest level of competition for athletes," Dot declared. "This one will always be remembered as an opportunity for us to not only represent our country and sport but all women athletes who were not given a chance."

After the Olympics

Two days after the gold medal game, Dot reported to the hospital for work. Instead of patients, Dr. Dot was greeted by a college marching band, 800 well-wishers, and flashing cameras. She also found out that the hospital had granted her another week off to visit the White House and celebrate with her teammates on the *Late Show with David Letterman* and at Disney World.

The Olympic win has made Dot more driven than ever to touch lives through medicine and softball, her two great interests. Now Dr. Shortstop has two new dreams—to win the gold in the 2000 Olympics and to open a large sports medicine complex in Florida. Her schedule still overflows with speaking engagements, volunteer work, and year-round camps and clinics. That's in addition to hospital rounds, California Commotion games, and wins with the international team. Dot Richardson is the only orthopedic surgeon who can claim 14 gold medals in national competition, her own signed bat (Louisville) and glove (Rawlings), a Dr. Dot watch, and eight other endorsement contracts as well as be spokesperson for the ASA and the new Women's Pro Softball League. The woman is a human dynamo.

"Dottie is testing herself on every level," Coach Enquist explains. "Nobody has made more of an impression on softball than Dot Richardson."

DOT'S OTHER INTERESTS:
Watching movies; traveling.

DOT'S SOFTBALL TIP:
Play the sport for the love of it. And play the sport the way you would love to watch it be played.

Chapter Four

Lisa Fernandez

Softball has many women stars. But none top the number of records held by Lisa Fernandez. In no-hitters, runs scored, and hits, this powerhouse pitcher leads the pack. Whether on a college, league, or national team, Lisa has been one of the most celebrated softball players in history.

"Usually you have the best hitter or pitcher," UCLA coach Sue Enquist stresses. "They are never the same person, like with Lisa Fernandez."

Always Daring

Lisa was born in 1971 in the small community of Long Beach, California—near a ball field. Lisa often accompanied her mother, Emilia Fernandez, to the park where a group of moms played slow-pitch. At two years, Lisa grabbed a paddle tennis racket and started swinging like her mother swung a bat. Even then, her arm impressed a passing photographer. The next day, the local paper ran Lisa's picture with the caption: "Like mom always said, keep your eye on the ball."

Besides having good coordination and a strong arm, little Lisa was very daring. She jumped into a pool before she could swim. She often talked to strangers, which drove her mother crazy. And she loved anything active, riding two-wheeled bikes and skating younger than most preschoolers.

"If anybody got into something, it would be Lisa," her mother laughed.

Of all the activities, Lisa liked softball best. By age five, she could throw a ball underhand and over-hand as well as catch and hit. She had talent, and she had the support of a softball-loving family. Both Emilia and Antonio, Lisa's father, played in park leagues. Her father had played amateur baseball on a company-sponsored team in his former homeland of Cuba. Her mother, who was born in Puerto Rico, also coached her older sister Elsie's team. Their live-in grandmother, Candida Padilla, gave a dollar to any girl on the team who hit a home run.

"Lisa wanted to join a team so bad," her mother said. "When she was five, we said she was six to get her on a start-up team."

Early Pitches

When Lisa was eight, she played slow-pitch. A coach for the Little Miss Softball Winter Ball League saw her at first base. He invited her to join his fast-pitch team. Lisa had never pitched before, but he needed a pitcher.

"My mom didn't want me to pitch because the mound was only 27 feet away, too close to the hitters," Lisa recalled. "But I told her I wanted to be where the coach wanted me." Eventually, Lisa's mother gave in, and Lisa learned fast-pitch.

After a few practices, another coach asked Lisa to start as pitcher for the team. Lisa was big for her age, and had a strong arm. He thought she was ready to test her skills. One week into the season, she pitched her first game. The team lost 20–0.

"I probably pitched to 20 batters and walked 20 batters," Lisa admitted. "My parents were very supportive. They said you have to work on getting one step better from now on. The next time on the mound, I walked 18, then 15, then 10, until I improved little by little. Later that year, we played the same team. We lost by only 1–0."

Softball and More

Lisa was determined at a young age to try her best in whatever she did. "My dad came from Cuba in the late 1950s with nothing and developed everything we have. He was a great role model—that fight and drive, that knowing nothing comes easy. He showed me that you have to do something right or not at all."

Lisa learned well. At Collins Elementary School, she was an honor student who shone in math. She liked to ask questions, and she liked to analyze problems. These qualities helped her in the classroom and with sports, which now included basketball, kickball, and softball.

Lisa's mother coached both daughters' softball teams. She also would catch for Lisa to help her improve her pitching skills. As Lisa got older, however, her pitches got faster. "By the time she was eleven, I needed all the gear—pads, mitt, and face mask—because I was scared of the ball. I had to protect myself," Ms. Fernandez recalled.

At eleven years old, Lisa made her first traveling team, which played in other towns. Lisa encountered more competition on this team. The team sponsor fueled competition by telling the girls they could earn college scholarships. Lisa thrived on the competition. It helped her focus on practicing and winning. It pushed her to stretch her skills to the limits.

"Ever since she was little, anything that meant competition Lisa did," her mother said.

Wins and Losses

The first year on the traveling team, Lisa helped win the league championship. Lisa pitched, easily placing balls to force batters out. The next year, she pitched another tournament win. Lisa found softball to be so much fun, she dropped volleyball, her other favorite sport at Alondra Junior High.

"By then, I knew I wanted to be a pitcher," Lisa said. "I didn't want to risk an injury from spiking and other moves in volleyball."

The winter after her second twelve-and-under team win, Lisa got a chance to try out for a fifteen-and-under team. Anyone who wanted to pitch for the team needed to see a special pitching coach. After watching Lisa throw, the coach tried to discourage her from pitching.

"He told me, 'Your body is just not built to be a pitcher. Your arms are too short,'" Lisa remembered. "No one ever told me that before. I was crushed."

On the way home, Lisa heard words that would always stay with her. Her mother warned her never to let someone else take away her dreams. If Lisa hoped to pitch, her mother said, she should follow her dream.

Lisa started on the fifteen-and-under team in the outfield. But she practiced pitching on her own whenever she could. As one of the younger players, Lisa had to prove herself. She worked her way from right field to second base to third base. Finally, the coach let her pitch for a game against the best team in the league, the Panthers. Lisa's team lost by only 1–0. A week later, the Panthers coach, Larry Mays, called to ask if Lisa would join his team the next season—as pitcher and third base person. Lisa was thrilled.

That season, the Panthers took first place in the nationals. They topped the league for two more years with Lisa as one of the starting pitchers. By then, the teenager was greeting reporters like a pro. She was becoming a local hero.

High School Days

Lisa's parents sent her to a small Catholic high school. "She needed more structure as a student," her mother explained. "We wanted her to concentrate on studies, not just athletics."

Lisa turned into a well-rounded teenager. At St. Joseph's, she made the basketball and softball teams while earning honor roll grades. She was still a people person, attracting lots of friends with her easygoing sense of humor. At home, she often listened to music and watched videos. All the while, she continued with the eighteen-and-under Panthers softball team.

Lisa had a great first year pitching with her school team, the St. Joseph Jesters. The Jesters went to the finals, pitting Lisa against the future professional pitcher Dee Dee Wieman.

"My freshman year I had a game that we won in 29 innings," Lisa recalled. "The game lasted 21 innings the first day and 8 the second. Dee Dee from Gahr High School and I were pitching rivals. We had 101 strikeouts between the two of us for the longest game in history."

That first season, Lisa's high school pitching earned her the first of many honors, Athlete of the Year in the Lakewood Hall of Fame. Each year, the mayor's office in nearby Lakewood and the local McDonald's, which houses the hall, asked area high schools and colleges to nominate outstanding student athletes. Judges chose one student from all the names to feature in a special display. Athlete of the Year grew into a big deal in Lakewood. In 1986, Lisa was thrilled to be part of the exhibit, one that now includes her practice jersey, bat, glove, and Olympic cleats.

Basketball and Other Successes

The Jesters made the playoffs each of Lisa's four years at St. Joseph's. The team won her freshman and senior years, lost in the quarters her second year, and went to semifinals her third year. By graduation, Lisa had pitched 60 shutouts and broken 20 southern California league records.

"She was such a gifted athlete," said softball coach Debbie Haley. "She is the only student at St. Joseph's who had a letter retired, number 16."

Basketball was another story. Although Lisa succeeded with the game, the team never won a championship. "I played basketball to give me something different," Lisa remembered. "I loved the fast action. In softball, it's one-on-one, the pitcher against the hitter. In basketball, you run plays around each other."

On to College

Lisa was good enough to receive a basketball scholarship for college. But softball was her first love. She knew that the University of California in Los Angeles (UCLA) was the number one women's softball team in the nation. When UCLA came calling, Lisa jumped at the chance to play with the greats. UCLA turned out to be perfect match for Lisa. She earned top grades, and she shone in softball.

"I have never seen anybody who worked so hard at her craft in my 20 years of coaching," Coach Enquist stressed. "Lisa was willing to come in so early before practice and stay so late to work on every part of the game. Her drive was unmatched. She came to compete and win."

Lisa was a four-time All-American. She led the Bruins to two first-place national championships (1990, 1992) and two second-place finishes (1991, 1993). In addition, she was the first softball player to receive the celebrated Honda-Broderick Cup, which goes to the most outstanding female college athlete of any sport. And she won the Honda Award for being a top student three times.

By the time Lisa left college, she had broken seven UCLA records for season and career pitches and hits. Moreover, she rewrote national college record books with her awesome numbers. In her senior year alone, Lisa led the nation in batting (.510) and earned-run average (0.25). Overall, she pitched an amazing 93 wins and 7 losses, logging a .930 winning percentage. She pitched 42 straight victories and 97 scoreless innings in a row with a 0.22 career earned-run average.

"Lisa will go down in UCLA history as the most successful player who put softball above and beyond where it was at the time," Coach Enquist emphasized. "Previously, the media never covered softball athletes. With her incredible accomplishments, the media was drawn to that success. She lifted UCLA softball to a new level."

Unexpected Challenges

Meanwhile, Lisa was picking up softball honors out-side of school. She played her first winning women's world championship with the U. S. national team in 1990. The following year, she pitched for the national team that won the Pan-American Games gold medal. Her skilled playing brought Lisa added media attention. For her talents, Lisa received the first endorsement from an athletic shoe company ever offered to a woman softball player.

Most national team action—about fifty games a season—happened between June and August. As the 1996 Olympics drew closer, however, the U.S. team required more time of their athletes. Practice and tournaments began to conflict with college. Lisa found she needed a break from her studies to focus on her game. The university supported her choice, allowing her to take fewer classes. Lisa graduated in 1995 with a degree in psychology, the study of how people behave.

At age twenty-four, Lisa was thrown a curve ball. Something happened during tryouts for the 1995 Pan-American team. Perhaps it was being away from a regular training and exercise program that the UCLA team had provided. Maybe being out of shape contributed to her poorer than usual performance on the field. Still, Lisa never expected to be slated for the USA Softball "B" club instead of the top "A" team. Now, she worried about her chances of making the 15-player Olympic team.

"It was a wake-up call to what life is all about," Lisa told the *Connecticut Post*. "You can't take anything for granted. I chose to be a pitcher because the ball is in your hand. It's up to you to perform at the top of your game—always."

> "You can't take anything for granted.... It's up to you to perform at the top of your game—always."

At first, the news threw her. How could people doubt her abilities? Then she began to doubt herself. She worried about her game. For the first time, she thought about leaving softball for good. After much thinking, however, Lisa decided to give softball one last push.

As before, she met the challenge with more practice and harder pitching. The extra work paid off. On the "B" team, Lisa pitched a no-hitter, a perfect game, and an amazing 0.511 at bat. She proved—to herself and the Olympic committee—that she still had the makings of a champion. In September, she made the top national team once again.

"For Lisa, being left out was a motivator," her mother explained. "She said, 'Okay, I'll show them they if don't think I'm good enough.' She was driven after that."

The Olympics

Lisa only pitched in three of the nine 1996 Olympic games. The one that really stood out for her was the game with Australia. She pitched a perfect eight

Lisa fiercely guards third base at the 1996 Olympics.

innings, and the United States scored one run. Near the end of the ninth inning, Australia had two strikes, two outs, and a runner on base. Then the worst happened. The Australian batter hit a home run, bringing in two runs. Australia beat the United States 2–1.

The game was the only U.S. loss. Still, Lisa felt *she* lost the game, maybe the gold medal. But she bounced back fighting during the game before the finals against China. With Lisa pitching, the Chinese never hit a ball past the infield until the seventh inning. Lisa held off run-ins with 66-mile-an-hour fastballs, finishing with 12 strikeouts and only three hits. In the tenth inning, Sheila Cornell batted a bases-loaded single, scoring the only game run for the U.S. 1–0 win.

The U.S. team met China again for the final gold medal game. Lisa never expected to pitch, knowing that honor went to Michele Granger. Lisa took third base as usual. But Michele ran into trouble in the sixth inning. With two outs, runners on second and third, and China's hardest hitter at bat, the U.S. coach called for Lisa to pitch.

Eighty-five hundred flag-waving fans went wild as the tough twenty-five-year-old approached the mound. China stole a run home, but Lisa blew away the batter with her sharp shots. The excited pitcher leaped into the air and beat her fists together, pumping up the crowd. Then she calmly struck out another three of four batters. Dot Richardson clinched the gold with a two-run home run. Lisa jumped into the arms of catcher Gillian Boxx as the United States won 3–1.

> *"The feeling you get from being an Olympic athlete is so overwhelming."*

"Her ability to play with such control in a pressure-packed situation proved once again that she has been the backbone of softball for so many years," Coach Enquist said.

The best part of the Olympics for Lisa came after the game. She accepted her gold medal with her teammates, which was the peak of her long, successful athletic career.

"The feeling you get from being an Olympic athlete is so overwhelming," Lisa admitted. "The pride in our country it brings out. I was somewhat sentimental because I knew my father had joined the army to fight for his country and what he believed in. And here I was in the arena I could be in, winning through sports."

Life After the Olympics

After the Olympics, Lisa took a year off to enjoy the fruits of her hard work. Her name appeared on knee pads and a glove and bat. One of her backers formed a Lisa Fernandez fan club, complete with a Web site. Lisa ran clinics and scheduled speaking engagements and public appearances. At every gathering, she brought her gold medal for others to see. She wanted everyone to celebrate the victory with her.

Once the Olympics excitement settled down, Lisa returned to UCLA. This time, she helped coach a new batch of Bruins. During her time off, she continued to host training camps and clinics. "I want to work with others to help them be the best they can be," she emphasized.

Then Lisa started to prepare for the next Olympics. She knew better than to take being on the Olympic team for granted. She joined the California Commotion women's team and trained with the national team. Off-season, she played with Team Toyota in Japan.

"Our women's division doesn't play lots of games," Lisa explained. "Playing overseas helps me sharpen my skills so I would be ready to compete."

Once again, the extra effort paid off. During the 63rd National Women's Major Fastpitch Tournament, the Commotion clobbered the Jazz 10–0. Tournament directors selected Lisa as most valuable player, an honor she has received three times. Lisa was named ASA Sportswoman of the Year twice and became a two-time Bertha Tickey Award winner. This recognition goes to the best pitcher in a women's national tournament.

Based on past performance, Lisa's fans can expect her to continue receiving awards for some time. She has been with the U.S. team for ten gold-winning international competitions and has no plans to stop making great plays.

As Commotion coach Kirk Walker told the *Connecticut Post*: "Her motto has always been to be the best she could be. I personally don't believe we've seen how good Lisa can be yet."

LISA'S OTHER INTERESTS:

Settling in her new home, taking care of her mother and father, coaching at UCLA, and focusing on the 2000 Olympics.

 ## LISA'S SOFTBALL TIP:

Go for your dreams and never be satisfied. Never allow someone else to limit you. You create your own limits. You can achieve anything you want in life.

Chapter Five

Julie Croteau

I n 1987, a student named Sue Perabo became the first woman to play baseball on a men's college team at Webster University. The following year, another coed added to baseball history. Julie Croteau swung a bat with St. Mary's College men for three years (1988–90). Then Julie broke new ground as the first woman to coach men's college baseball. From men's college ball to the women's professional Silver Bullets to the men's semipros, Julie kept batting down barriers so everyone would know that modern girls can and do play baseball.

Just for Fun

Julie was born on December 4, 1970, in Berkeley, California. Her parents, Ray and Nancy Croteau, moved their baby to Manassas, Virginia, where Julie grew up. Ray and Nancy were lawyers and not very interested in baseball. But they believed in sports for Julie and her younger sister, Nicole. They agreed to support the girls wherever their interests took them.

Ray tossed balls with young Julie until she learned to catch. Then Julie and her cousin John spent hours outdoors playing ball. He threw balls at her as hard as he could. Julie always caught the ball.

At age five, Julie began playing T-ball with the Little League. That was just two years after girls had won the right to play in Little League. At the time, half of Julie's teammates were girls. And Julie finished the season with a sure .300 batting average. Yet, she still heard what would become a familiar refrain: "Baseball is a boy's game. Softball is for girls."

"It seemed ridiculous to me," Julie stressed in *Women's Sports and Fitness*. "Softball and baseball are completely different sports. It almost became a thing where I refused to play softball because everyone told me to do it."

Getting Serious

The older Julie got, the fewer girls played on the Little League team. Like her friends, Julie tried ballet and other sports. But she was falling in love with baseball. In 1979, eight-year-old Julie sat in the bleachers at Boston's Fenway Park and announced to her parents, "I want to be a professional baseball player."

By age twelve, Julie was the only girl on her team. She also logged the second-highest batting average on the team. Most teammates treated her well. But some resented a girl on the team. When it came time to vote for the end-of-the-season all-star team, none voted for Julie.

The next summer, Julie's coaches sent her to the all stars. The following season, the pony-tailed first baseman moved up to the major league for ages thirteen to fifteen and played in another fall league for fourteen-year-olds. Off-season, she attended clinics and practiced constantly. But coaches took less time with her as she grew older. They figured a girl could never go any further with baseball. Still, Julie caught balls, got opponents out, and often hit game-winning balls. She would never be a powerhouse, but she was a solid player who worked her heart out to play.

High School

Julie went out for baseball her first year at Osbourn Park High School. She was only about 5 feet tall. She accepted that she wasn't quite good enough to make the team. After tryouts, the coach discussed softball with her, the first of many similar talks. "It's not my sport," she told him.

The next year she tried out again. She was 2 inches taller. Her skills had improved. She was a good player, and not just for a girl. Although the coach talked softball again, Julie made the junior varsity team. She hoped to play first base. The coach benched her most of the season.

"I felt like the coach was embarrassed having a girl on his team," Julie told one author. "Having a girl who could start would be a putdown on the school."

Returning for her third year, Julie found a different junior varsity coach. This man liked her playing. He had her lead warmups, assuring her a place on the team, possibly as captain. But the varsity coach interfered. In the end, Julie was cut. For the first time, she wondered if she was taking her desire to play baseball too far. Yet, she stubbornly refused to give up the game she loved.

Julie was sure she would make the varsity team her last year at Osbourn. The seniors had graduated, leaving 14 openings. She knew from the Babe Ruth League outside school that she was better than most of the guys. Still, Julie was cut again.

"The coach made the comment that no girl was going to play on his team," Ray Croteau explained. "The principal couldn't believe that a girl could make the team. I knew she should have made it." The family sued the coach and principal for keeping Julie from her rightful place on the team solely because she was a girl. Once news of a lawsuit leaked out, the media circus began.

Day in Court

At the trial, many Osbourn Yellow Jackets sided with their coach. Longtime friends spoke against Julie. Many felt they had to. Their baseball futures were at stake. Others sent a letter to the newspapers saying that they in no way backed Julie. "Not because she is female but because we feel this suit has no grounds.... Our job is to win baseball games (with) the best seventeen athletes." Newspapers rightly included the Yellow Jackets record. Their 4 wins, 13 losses, and 1 tie hardly supported the claim that the team fielded the "best seventeen athletes."

"When I went up there, it was evident what was going on," reporter Mike Zitz remembered. "The players were snickering in and out of the courtroom.

66

When I saw the tape in the courtroom with her footwork around first base and her bat work, it was obvious she could play at that level. The boys' problem was rooted in something other than her ability."

> *"The boys' problem was rooted in something other than her ability."*

For two weeks, Julie listened to her coach and teammates rip her apart. "They were saying: 'She can't run, she can't throw, she can't walk, she's horrible, she can't be on our team,'" Julie told *People Weekly*. "After that I was having a little trouble believing in myself."

Although some players, a college coach, and Babe Ruth coaches championed Julie's playing, her case never had a chance. The judge ruled that Julie had received a fair tryout. According to him, not making the team had nothing to do with Julie being a girl. When the judge dismissed the case, the coach and team cheered and jumped around like they had won the world series. Julie was heartbroken.

Outside the courtroom, she told Zitz she would keep practicing with her father. Then she broke down and cried. "I thought it was wrong that someone should love the game and have the ability and be booted out," Zitz said. He felt terrible. Then he thought of a way to help her. He invited Julie to practice with his semipro men's team, the Fredericksburg Giants.

Playing with the Big Boys

The lawsuit left Julie a target. "Guys put notes on my car. They made me feel bad in the hallway."

Luckily, Julie had more success with the Giants. She got two hits during her first practice game. After one hit, she was waved around third base to score at home plate. But the throw got there 10 feet ahead of her. Instead of giving up, the 5-foot, 7-inch, 130-pounder put her shoulder down and tried to bulldoze through the 200-pound catcher and knock the ball loose. She didn't, but Zitz realized she had the nerve to play against much bigger players. He waved the eighteen-year-old age rule to let her play. At age seventeen, Julie joined the semipro Giants.

Julie knew this was a chance of a lifetime. She drove 45 minutes each way just to practice. She was first to arrive and last to leave. "She was a solid player and really dedicated," Zitz reported. "Usually, Julie would be our number nine hitter. She had the ability to concentrate and focus. She handled pressure on the field. That's the kind of player you want to have."

> *"She had the ability to concentrate and focus. She handled pressure on the field. That's the kind of player you want to have."*

Still, many people on the team let the coach know they didn't want Julie there. The media gave her too much attention. At one hit for every nine, her batting average was low. "A lot of people left after the first season and criticized me in the paper," Zitz recalled. "They said I was trying to get attention for the team. But I had nothing to gain from it."

One pitcher and outfielder switched to another team. They refused to play with a girl. At the end of the season, the Giants wound up playing their team in the finals. In the eighth inning of a tie game, the former Giant's pitcher relieved the regular. Julie came up to bat. All the while, people kept screaming that Julie couldn't hit. She calmly smacked a line drive past the pitcher into left field. The ball bounced in front of the outfielder who opposed her playing, allowing a run in and Julie to make it to first base. Julie's single turned out to be the winning run in the game.

College Ball

All Julie wanted was a chance to play baseball in college. St. Mary's College in Maryland agreed to allow her to try out for the Seahawks, their National Collegiate Athletic Association (NCAA) Division III team. If she made the grade, she could play. Julie worked hard with the Seahawks through fall training. By spring, she had made the team.

Julie's opening game in March 1989 made national news. Fifteen cameras focused on the girl baseball player at first. Julie was nervous, but she easily fielded six balls. She batted three times and never made it to first base. She played like an average

Seahawk. The team lost to Spring Garden College 4–1. Afterward, Julie faced a flood of reporters.

"Not too many eighteen-year-olds could handle the media and audiences the way she did," Mike Zitz recalled. "Everything she said was well thought out and well reasoned."

Besides reporters, Julie made the rounds of television talk shows. NBC's *Today Show* named her Sportswoman of the Week. She received honors from women's groups for her bold step toward equality for girls. Julie thought reporters were making too much of her historic season. "But then I saw that it brought a lot of attention to girls playing baseball and to the women's baseball league in the 1950s," Julie told *Women's Sports and Fitness*. "Now other girls know it can be done today, so it's been a good thing."

By the end of Julie's first season at St. Mary's, she had connected with 10 hits in 45 at bat for a .222 average. She had made only 5 errors in 92 chances, a good record for a bottom-ranking Division III team with a 1-win, 20-loss record.

"Julie was tough," coach Hal Willard told *Sports Illustrated*. Several opposing coaches said there was no doubt she was a legitimate Division III player.

Too Much Boys Being Boys

The first two years at St. Mary's, Julie's teammates supported her being on the team. A few told her to watch for one player, but nothing came of that. As long as she played well, they knew she deserved to be there. By her third year, guys felt comfortable around her—sometimes too comfortable. A few read sexy magazines aloud or played tapes on the bus. Julie never admitted how much some of their bus talk about girls and sex offended her.

On the field, other teams had a hard time playing against a girl. Julie ignored much of the childishness. What she couldn't ignore, however, were the potshots at her. Her body caught more than her share of pitches during St. Mary's and Giants games.

"Other pitchers would say this girl is not going to get a hit off me," Zitz said. "They would overthrow and walk her. One time she got hit, and the pitch broke her ankle. A television camera panned the pitcher, and he was smiling."

By the end of Julie's first year at St. Mary's, she was no longer news. As the number of media decreased, so did her time on the field. The coach kept her in the dugout for much of her third year on the team.

Originally, Julie planned on going to law school. She cared about underdogs. She wanted to make sure other girls received a fairer chance at life than she had. By her third season of heckling, cruel jokes, and fighting for the right to play baseball, however, she was worn down. Julie took some time off from school to think about what she wanted to do.

A League of Their Own

In 1991, Julie was invited to a Women's Sports Foundation annual dinner honoring women athletes. This honor led to an internship with the foundation. While there, Julie learned about the All-American Girls Professional Baseball League (AAGPBL). For the first time, she felt less alone. Then she felt angry.

"I'd been playing baseball for 13 years without a single mention of early women ball players, never mind professionals," she admitted to a reunion of 160 former players. "I was mad because I had felt alone, which is okay when you are, but I wasn't. And I was mad for you ladies, because somewhere, somehow, you had been cheated out of your place in the history books."

Julie was delighted to learn that their story was being made into a movie called *A League of Their Own*. The movie's casting director heard about Julie's ball playing and called her to be part of the film. She gave Julie roles as a stunt double for actress Anne Ramsay and other characters. Julie wore different wigs so she could make fantastic saves at first base and center field.

After the movie, Julie returned to St. Mary's. This time she concentrated on her studies. She stayed off the college team but continued to practice with the Giants. She began giving clinics for young girls. She told them to "keep playing."

Playing with Girls

In 1992, Julie graduated with a degree in philosophy and a minor in Spanish. The next year she entered a program in exercise and sports studies at the all-women's Smith College. Her new dream was to coach baseball. On the side, she got a part-time job as assistant baseball coach at Western New England College in Springfield, Massachusetts. Once again, she made news, this time as the fiirst woman to coach men's college baseball.

"Julie worked on fielding," Gene Gumbs said. "She took what she did very seriously. *Good Morning America* filmed a segment one morning. But she didn't seem to want the attention. She wanted to coach and loved to share her knowledge of baseball."

In December 1993, Julie heard about the formation of the women's professional Silver Bullets. She was invited to a select tryout in Florida the following spring. Even though tryouts were in the middle of final exams at Smith College, Julie couldn't resist. She left her coaching job, packed her bags, and headed for spring training in Florida.

Julie and 49 other women lasted through the first cut. After a month of training and competing, Julie made the team of 24 players. She was the only member of the team who had never played baseball with girls.

"I've been through things people shouldn't have to go through to play a game," Julie reported in *The*

Sporting News. "I've had people spit on me, call me names, and call me in the middle of the night. This is the prize for not letting them get to me."

Julie thrilled Bullets fans and opponents with her skills at first base. At the end of the first season, she led the Silver Bullets in getting batters out from the field. She recorded an awesome .990 fielding percentage with only two errors in 29 games. She was one of only two hitters on the team with more walks than strikeouts. Julie gained a reputation for patience and a good eye.

Julie tosses the ball to first base to complete a play.

Bonus of Playing with the Bullets

Playing with the Silver Bullets led to an offer with the men's professional Maui Stingrays. Julie jumped at the chance to play with an accredited major league baseball winter league. In fall 1994, she and teammate Lee Ann Ketcham left for Hawaii. Here they found men from Japan, Korea, Hawaii, and elsewhere in the United States on the roster.

At first, they felt out of place. "Baseball brought everything together," Julie told *USA Today*. "When they see you're there to play, that you're not just there to date them, that you're not just there for the story, then you start to get some respect."

In the end, women felt they were given too little game time. After a season, Julie recorded 1 hit in only 12 at bat and no errors at first base.

The next season, Julie returned to the Silver Bullets. During practice, she injured her shoulder, which required surgery. Facing a long recovery, Julie stopped playing with the Silver Bullets. She also ended her long run with the Giants.

"Julie played with us on and off for about six years," Zitz stressed. "The league has a 15-year history, and she was our best first baseman."

New Directions

Julie was able to stay with the Silver Bullets as a television broadcaster. When the season ended, she returned to Smith College to finish her classes. While there, she coached at the nearby University of Massachusetts in Amherst. This job gave Julie another first, this time as assistant coach for an NCAA Division I team.

In the beginning, the players gave Julie a hard time, much like when she played on a men's team. But nothing seemed new to Julie. "I've found out the better the player, the more confidence they have in their ability, the easier it is to accept me."

Outside school, Julie pursued other ways to stay in baseball. She broadcasted games on radio and on television. She held clinics. Once school ended, she went to work for Major League Baseball, holding clinics and organizing games around the world. Whatever job she held, she tried to make things better for girls in sports. For her efforts, the National Baseball Hall of Fame added her glove and photo to a display in 1995.

"She is a very strong, caring person," Mike Zitz explained. "She is trying to reach out to younger girls who love baseball and have people who try to stop them from doing it. She hopes what she's doing makes a difference."

JULIE'S OTHER INTERESTS:
Sports, time with friends and family.

 ## JULIE'S BASEBALL TIP:
Keep playing.

Chapter Six

Ila Borders

Baseball girls find few outlets for their interests. They must fight for the chance to try out and play each game. No one has fought more baseball battles than Ila Borders. Not because she likes to make a fuss. Rather, Ila breaks down barriers because it is the only way she can continue to play the game she loves. From Little League to professional minor leagues, Ila has been a pioneer in modern women's baseball.

Born to Pitch

Ila was born on February 18, 1975 to Phil and Marianne Borders. She was their firstborn of four children—two girls and two boys. She was also their first lefty. Phil a former minor leaguer, thrilled to watch his baby struggle to clasp a spoon with her right hand but easily grab it with her left.

"My first thought was, 'left-handed pitchers don't grow on trees,'" her father told *The News-Times*.

Ila began playing catch with her dad when she was three. Before long, the catches turned into serious pitches. Ila couldn't wait to join the Little Miss Softball League in her hometown of La Mirada, California. By the time she was seven, Ila's throwing arm had developed an incredible reach for someone her age. She was one of the few kids on the team who could throw a ball from third to first base. Not surprisingly, the coach placed her at third.

The following season, Ila joined an all-star travel-ing team. Only the most talented players received an invitation to play. The all-stars competed year-round with three-day double-header tournaments most weekends. Ila never tired of softball. She couldn't get enough of the game.

Change of Heart

When Ila was ten, she attended a Dodgers game with her dad. She loved the excitement. She went crazy after seeing Dusty Baker hit a home run. When the game ended, Ila announced that she was through with softball. She wanted to play baseball and to pitch overhand.

Ila's mother brought her to sign up for Little League. The men never said girls couldn't be on the team. Instead, they told Ila's mother to bring more paperwork the next day. When the two came back with the papers, they discovered that registration had closed. This was the first of many slights Ila would experience during her long baseball career.

The men placed Ila's name on a waiting list. Three games into the season, a coach called Ila to play baseball. As soon as he saw her throw, he sent her to the pitcher's mound. Ila was delighted. But her first time pitching, she hit the batter—a scary way to begin a career.

Moving Up

Ila batted with the same force as she threw a ball. Her first time at bat, a long drive bounced off the centerfield fence for a double. A coach from the next highest Little League level ran to find out who cracked the bat. That swing gave Ila entry into the majors.

In 1985, not many girls joined Little League majors anywhere. At age ten, Ila was on her own with the La Habra boys. Her teammates accepted her because they knew she could play. But she was becoming a target for opposing pitchers. At one game, a pitcher shot two balls at her head. Ila never reacted. Instead, she hit a triple off the outfield wall her next time at bat.

"Ila and I had a heart-to-heart talk," her father wrote on Ila's Web site. "My feeling was that if she wanted to continue she would always have to work harder than any of the boys to be physically strong enough to be competitive. Ila understood this, and we spent the entire summer and winter working one-on-one on different aspects of the game."

Ila stayed on the majors team for the next two years. The following season, she made the majors all-stars, where she pitched the second postseason game (a 4–2 loss). She also joined a local park league in neighboring Whittier.

News about the girl pitcher from La Mirada was getting around. A television crew filmed part of her all-star game. That was the year the team made it to district and sectional levels. Ila pitched a wonderful game, even with reporters taking notes. She discovered she could easily focus while under the pressure of being in the spotlight.

Junior High Dreams

By age thirteen, Ila began hearing more calls for her to return to softball. Critics claimed the boys were getting too big and strong. They assumed she couldn't keep up. But Ila rode the baseball bandwagon to new levels during her junior high years. At Whittier Christian Junior High, the normally shy girl asked to try out with 60 boys for one of 20 positions on the baseball team. That request made her the only girl to try out in the 16 years Coach Rolland Esslinger coached at the school. Moreover, she became the only girl to make the team.

"For that age, her speed was above average, and she had a really good curve ball," Coach Esslinger noted. "She spotted her pitches well, and her slow pitches were wicked—hard for hitters to hit. She was smart and knew where to throw the ball and what would get hitters out."

Coach Esslinger worked hard to keep the spotlight off Ila. The boys had no problem with a girl on their team. Everyone changed into uniforms before they went anywhere, so locker rooms were never a concern. For her part, Ila practiced beyond what the team did. She was determined to perform well, which she did. Most parents and fans approved of her on the team.

"She had proved herself such a good player that she wasn't viewed as a joke," the coach reported. "But some of the teams we played had a hard time because she was a girl. That age group of boys thought it wasn't good to get struck out by a girl."

In eighth grade, Ila pitched a shutout during a championship game against Pasadena Christian School. Whittier won 10–1, with one run scored by stealing bases. Afterward, the team voted Ila most valuable player for the second season.

Ila left Whittier with pitching and hitting records that still stand today. She also moved up to the Little League senior division and played on another town league. On Sundays, she joined her father's team as pitcher. Here she got her first taste of playing the game with men.

With all these teams, Ila averaged six games a week, a punishing schedule. Often, she changed jerseys in the car between games. All this baseball taught Ila to pace herself. She also realized that she wanted to play professional ball. Ila started saving money to visit the National Baseball Hall of Fame in Cooperstown.

High School Choices

Ila was a good student and an all-around athlete. She hoped to continue baseball into high school, if she made the team. To make sure Ila received a chance, her dad called the local high school coach. Once again, Ila's father heard that his daughter could never make it to the next level. Ila parents sent her to a private school, Whittier Christian High School, instead.

Ila easily made the Whittier freshman baseball team. A few months into the season, the coach bumped her up to the next level team. By the end of the season, Ila played on the varsity team, the highest level. Her parents' belief in her dream had paid off.

"Whittier gave her the chance, and she did the rest," her father wrote.

Ila continued to hear that she didn't belong. That only made her work harder, trying to ignore the insults and swears directed at her during games. Meanwhile, adults criticized her parents for allowing a girl to play with teenage boys and grown men.

Scouting for Ila

The local newspaper followed Ila's baseball career with many articles. Umpires spread the word about what a good pitcher she was. Several college coaches began appearing at Whittier to watch her pitch. In Ila's third year, she signed with Southern California College, a small Christian college of 900 students in Costa Mesa.

"I brought her to our school and told her to throw a couple balls," Charlie Phillips, former Southern California coach, recalled. "I had her pitch against my top lineup. She only gave up one run in three innings. She was tough mentally on the field."

With college decided, Ila could relax and enjoy her last year in high school. She kept up her grades, had fun with friends, and played basketball in addition to baseball. She proved a good athlete in whatever she tried, averaging 10 to 12 points a basketball game.

Baseball was where Ila shone, however. She graduated in 1993 with an overall record of 16 wins and 7 losses. Teammates voted her most valuable player her senior year.

College Baseball

Ila pitched her first game at Southern California the fall of her freshman year. She threw 104 pitches against Claremont-Mudd for nine innings, helping her team win 12–1. With this game, the pony-tailed athlete made history. Ila became the first female to pitch a complete game for a men's college team. When the game ended, Ila had several strikeouts and many new fans.

"You've got to respect her," Claremont second baseman Gabe Rosenthal told a reporter. "After she was getting everybody out, I think people realized she was just another pretty good baseball player and forgot she was a girl."

The game caused a huge uproar. More than 300 television camera crews, photographers, and reporters from around the world lined the field. After the game, the media circus continued. Ila's picture adorned the front of Japanese sports pages. She received invitations for several television talk shows. Ila agreed to so many interviews that her B-average grades dropped to Cs.

As a result of the game, the National Baseball Hall of Fame asked Ila for her Southern California jersey, baseball, and cap. The items became part of the permanent exhibit about "Women in Baseball."

"I began saving money when I was twelve just to be able to go," Ila told a reporter. "Now to be displayed there blows my mind."

Second Year Changes

Ila's grades picked up her second year, but her pitching declined. Part of the reason was that the coach decided Ila needed a new way of pitching, which took time to learn. Ila ended the season with 1 win and 7 losses.

"She uses her head to find hitters' weaknesses," Coach Phillips explained. "She didn't have a good year. But we didn't have a good team to back her up, either."

The slump renewed calls against a woman in college baseball. Teammates grew unhappy with all the attention Ila was getting. Other teams had their own problems. One coach threatened to pull his team if Ila pitched. Batters didn't want to lose to a lady. The swears and abuse hurled at Ila turned nastier. Some of the insults hurt Ila. Usually, she tried to block them out.

Most people assumed Ila could never pitch professional baseball. Without her dad, they figured she couldn't handle the heat. Coach Phillips arranged for Ila to pitch with the Canadian Swift Current Indians during the summer before her third year. He wanted to toughen her up and give her professional experience. Ila spent the summer improving her skills. She would show baseball scouts she could survive on her own.

A New School

Ila returned from Canada to find a new coach at Southern California. She pitched several preseason games with good results. But the coach told Ila she had lost her place as starting pitcher. He also kept asking her when she was switching schools. Ila spent most of the season benched.

Even then, the abuse continued. Ila could take the swearing and insults. But some teammates tried to hurt her. One day, she was filling up a bucket with balls in the outfield.

"I turned my back, and they just rifled balls as hard as they could from about 30 feet," Ila told

"I can't let them get the best of me."

60 Minutes. "They nailed me in the back. I had welts all over me. My roommate was like, 'What in the heck are you doing this for?' And I'd go, 'I can't let them get the best of me.'"

86

The combination of bullying and not playing got to be too much. Ila transferred to Whittier College during her last year. There she started to have fun playing baseball again. The Whittier coach sent her in for 81 innings. She wound up the season with 4 wins and 5 losses. More important, the school provided the support she lacked at Southern California.

Blazing New Trails

In May 1996, the coach for the St. Paul Saints, an independent minor league team, invited Ila to tryouts. The 5-foot 10-inch lefty competed for two weeks against 22 other players for a spot on the team. Ila pitched her first preseason game against the Duluth-Superior Dukes.

"She struck out our first batter," said Dukes owner Jim Wadley. "It went from a joke on the bench to a very serous pitcher who was throwing strikes. I watched her for two days—her conduct, posture, handling of the press and the crowds. I told the Saints manager that if he doesn't sign her, I'm interested."

In the end, the Saints signed Ila. Some grumbled it was a publicity stunt. Her fastball only clocked at 83 mph. But Marty Scott, the Saints manager, thought Ila had good control over the ball. She could change speeds easily. Besides, he liked her work ethic and the way she played.

Ila's opening appearance left many doubting Scott's choice. Ila hit a batter and threw a wild ball to first. The Sioux Falls Canaries earned three runs without an out. The next two outings, Ila rallied before adoring crowds. Still, within a month, Scott traded Ila to the Dukes.

New Kid on the Block

Usually, coaches used Ila as a relief pitcher. She went into the game when a win or loss was certain. Between her first run with the St. Paul Saints and midseason trade to the Dukes, she made 21 relief appearances on the mound. She had no errors and recorded a 7.20 earned-run average (ERA) the first season and 7.53 ERA the second, not pro numbers but a good start.

Almost from Ila's first day, the Dukes' game changed. Ila brought her over-the-top work habits to the team, raising the levels of teammates. Even though she didn't pitch much, her conduct seemed to affect how teammates played.

"She ran farther, stretched more, and exercised harder and longer than most players," Wadley recalled. "It was almost as if they saw her doing it and thought that a girl can't outdo me. When Ila came to the team in 1997, we had 4 wins and 17 losses. Then we went on to win the Northern League championship that year. If you combine Ila's first season—one month with St. Paul and the two months with us—you get the best record in the league."

More reporters followed Dukes games because the team had a *girl* now. After each game, the media mobbed Ila. With all the attention, attendance skyrocketed. Packs of young fans shouted her name at games and crowded around their new hero for her autograph.

Rather than make a statement about women in baseball, Ila simply wanted to play baseball and fit in. Mostly, Ila succeeded in practicing and training like everyone else. Making friends on the team proved more difficult, however. Ila made a point of not partying with teammates. After practices or games, she went back to her hotel room. On bus trips, she read or listened to music. She dressed and showered by herself at home or in her hotel room. She rarely entered the locker room with the other players. All this left her lonely most of the time.

"So much happens in here, like when guys talk," one Duke revealed. "This is where the bonding takes place. It's hard for her to bond with us because she can't really come in here."

Playing with the Dukes

In her second season with the Dukes, Ila won a place on the starting lineup. On July 9, 1998, she became the first woman named as starting pitcher in a regular season minor league game. More than 2,200 fans and CNN, ESPN, and Japanese reporters watched history take place.

Ila's firm pitching form reveals her fierce determination.

Ila gave them a good show. Going into the fifth inning, she posted a 2–1 lead against the Sioux Falls Canaries. Then two batters hit home runs off her. Ila threw 71 pitches before the Dukes lost 8–3. This was the longest run in her 23-appearance professional career. Despite the loss, Ila's historic start was called a success.

One month later, Ila made history again. On July 24, 1998, she became the first woman to pitch a winning game in a men's professional league. She kept the Sioux Falls Canaries from scoring for six innings, recording a 3–1 win for the Dukes.

"All they have to do is give her the chance, and she'll win them over," reporter Roger Murray noticed.

Moving On

After the year at Whittier, Ila returned to Southern California to complete her college degree in teaching physical education. Off-season, she worked in her mother's daycare center or was a substitute teacher at schools. In between work, she pushed herself to stay in shape by throwing balls, batting, running, and exercising.

Ila remained with the Dukes until the 1999 season. Then she was traded to the Madison Black Wolfs. She didn't mind. She was ready for a fresh start on a team that would use her more.

At the time, Madison was in last place. Unlike Ila's earlier teams, the Wolfs put her in the regular lineup. She pitched the first three innings of every game. Finally, she felt part of a team.

By the end of the summer, she had the team's lowest turnaround average (1.76). The Wolfs had won 65 percent of their games. The last-place team now led the second half of the league. When the season ended, the Black Wolfs were one game short of the playoffs, and Ila had had a good season.

Even after years of pro pitching, Ila is still considered an oddity in baseball. And she still receives her share of hard knocks. Most of what Ila goes through has little to do with her pitching ability.

She's put down because she's a girl invading a boys' game—plain and simple. Yet, Ila seems satisfied no matter where baseball takes her—teaching, coaching, or the pros.

"Sometimes, I can't believe what I'm doing," Ila exclaimed. "I'm living a dream. I'm playing professional baseball on a great team. I have great support. This is so amazing that everything is happening basically the way I wanted it to happen since I was ten years old."

ILA'S OTHER INTERESTS:
Almost any sports, reading, writing, being with kids.

ILA'S BASEBALL TIP:
Keep focused. Work harder than anyone else. Perseverance is the key in all sports.

Baseball and Softball Talk

Glossary

ball   a pitch, at which the batter never swings, that passes outside the strike zone

base   one of four points on the baseball diamond that a runner must touch to be safe

batter   the player who tries to hit the pitched ball with a bat

batting order   list that shows which batter bats first, second, third, and so on

catcher   the defending player who stands behind home plate and catches balls the batter does not hit

fair territory   the area outside the baseball diamond that is still part of the playing field

fast pitch   type of pitch that is thrown with great speed

foul ball   a ball that lands outside the baseball diamond and fair territory

home plate   starting and ending point at the lower corner of the baseball diamond

home run   a hit that allows the batter to circle the bases and score a run

infield   the area of the playing field that is inside the baseball diamond

outfield   the area of the playing field that extends outward from the baseball diamond

pitcher   the defending player who throws, or pitches, the ball to the batter

shortstop   the defending player who tries to catch hit balls that come between second and third base

steal   a runner's successful run to the next base when there is no batted ball

strike   occurs when a batter either hits the ball into foul territory, out-of-bounds, or swings and misses the ball; three strikes and a batter is out

strike zone   the space that parallels the area between the batter's mid-chest and top of the knees where the ball should be pitched so the batter can hit it

walk   occurs when a batter advances to first base after receiving four pitches that were called as balls

Baseball and Softball Connections

Where to Find More Information

Baseball/Softball Groups for Women and Girls

The Amateur Softball Association
USA Softball
2801 NE 50th
Oklahoma City, Oklahoma 73130
(405) 425-3463
www.softball.org

This group is the national governing body for softball that sets rules, organizes teams, and selects softball greats for the National Softball Hall of Fame in Oklahoma City.

Women's Pro Softball League
(formerly Women's Pro Fastpitch)
90 Madison Street, Suite 200
Denver, Colorado 80206
(303) 316-7800
www.prosoftball.com

This four-year-old league organizes a 66-game regular season with six teams and publishes the magazine *Riseball*.

National Baseball Hall of Fame and Museum
25 Main Street
P.O. Box 590
Cooperstown, New York 13326
(607) 547-7200
www.baseballhalloffame.org
This is a wonderful place located in a town that looks like a turn-of-the-century Main Street. Cooperstown oozes baseball.

General Sports for Women and Girls

**National Association for Girls
and Women in Sports**
1900 Association Drive
Reston, Virginia 20191-1599
703-476-3452
www.aahperd.org/nagws.html
The NAGWS has been fighting to promote females in sports since 1899. Members helped pass Title IX and sponsor National Girls and Women in Sports Day, February 4th. Be sure to celebrate the day by playing your favorite sport!

Women's Sports Foundation
Eisenhower Park
East Meadow, New York 11554
(800) 227-3988
(516) 542-4700
www.lifetimetv.com/wosport/index.htm
This group distributes education guides, videos, general sports information, and lists of scholarships and awards, including its International Women's Sports Hall of Fame.

Canadian Association for the Advancement of Women and Sport and Physical Activity

1600 James Naismith Drive
Gloucester, ON, Canada, K1B 5N4
(613) 748-5793
caaws@caaws.ca

This group is the Canadian version of the Women's Sports Foundation. They have up-to-date information about girls' and women's programs for every sport in Canada.

Girls Incorporated

120 Wall Street
New York, New York 10005-3902
(212) 509-2000
www.girlsinc.org

This organization runs programs to help girls become stronger, smarter, and bolder. Contact them for information about a given sport and starting programs in your area.

U.S. Olympic Committee

1 Olympic Plaza
Colorado Springs, Colorado 80909
(719) 632-5551
www.olympic.usa.org

These people have the scoop about the Olympics, Olympic camps, and how to get involved.

Big Ten Conference

1500 West Higgins Road
Park Ridge, Illinois 60068-6300
(847) 696-1010
www.bigten.org

This association coordinates girls' and boys' sports at Big Ten universities. One of its special information and activity programs for younger girls is Dream Big. Big Ten offers a free kit for helping young girls and coaches start programs for different sports and keep them going.

Girl Scouts of USA
420 Fifth Avenue
New York, New York 10018
(212) 852-8000
misc@gsusa.org

Girls Scouts has a national program called GirlSports, for girls ages five to seventeen. They hold sport leadership and national summer sports events and sponsor health and fitness activities. Contact them for sports posters, coloring books, and diaries.

YWCA of the USA
726 Broadway
5th Floor
New York, New York 10003
(212) 614-2858

This pioneer organization for girls' and women's fitness and sport programs is the only group to hold a seat on the U.S. Olympic Committee.

National Organization for Women
1000 16th Street, NW, Suite 700
Washington, DC 20036
(202) 331-0066
www.now.org

This national organization will represent anyone in court who feels unfairly excluded from playing a sport because of being a girl. They argued the landmark case that opened Little League to girls.

Staying Hot
Further Reading

Hanmer, Trudy. *The All-American Girls Professional Baseball League*. New York: New Discovery Books, 1994.

Healy, Dennis. *The Illustrated Rules of Baseball*. Nashville, TN: Ideals, 1995. This is baseball at its easiest for beginners.

Macy, Sue. *A Whole New Ball Game*. New York: Henry Holt, 1993. Interesting story of the All-American Girls Professional Baseball League.

Proboz, Kathilyn. *The Girls Strike Back: The Making of the Pink Parrots*. Waltham, MA: Little Brown, 1990. Fiction story about junior high girls who want their own baseball team.

Richardson, Dot, and Yeager, Don. *Living the Dream*. New York: Kensington Books, 1997. Easy-to-read autobiography.

Sammons, Barry, and Fernandez, Lisa. *Fastpitch Softball: The Windmill Pitcher*. Indianapolis: Masters Press, 1997. Lisa's how-to book.

Bibliography

Books

Berlage, Gai Ingham. *Women in Baseball: The Forgotten History*. Westport, CT: Praeger, 1999.

Burke, Larry. *The Baseball Chronicles*. New York: Michael Friedman Publishing, 1996.

Frommer, Harvey. *Growing Up at Bat*. New York: Pharos Books, 1989.

Gregorich, Barbara. *Women at Play: The Story of Women in Baseball*. San Diego, CA: Harcourt Brace & Company, 1993.

Hood, John. *Why They Scratch Themselves: How to Understand Baseball*. Tinley Park, IL: Forward Press, 1994.

Johnson, Susan. *When Women Played Hardball*. Seattle, WA: Seal Press, 1994.

Martinez, David. *The Book of Baseball Literacy*. New York: Penguin, 1986.

Rader, Benjamin. *Baseball: A History of America's Game*. Urbana, IL: University of Illinois Press, 1992.

Web Sites

Dare to Compete: biographies of famous women in sports
http://www.hbo.com/dare/

Ila's Bio
http://www.ilaborders.com

All-American Girls Professional Baseball League
http://www.dlcwest.com

Rules of Baseball
http://www.majorleaguebaseball.com

the go, girl! plan: Softball Rules of the Game
http://www.gogirlmag.com/backiss/backiss18/prog.htm

Women in Baseball by Debra Shattuck
http://www.totalbaseball.com/history/group/
women/women.html

Notable Years of Women in Baseball
http://www.lifetimetv.co/sports/silver_bullets/
women.html

Just the Facts/Profile
http://www.drshortstop.com

Dot Richardson articles
http://archives.orlandosentinel.com

Lisa Fernandez Fan Club
http://members.aol.com/lisa16usa

Articles

Egan, Erin. "Toni Stone was one of the only women ever to play pro baseball with men."*Sports Illustrated for Kids,* April 1994, v. 6, n. 4, p. 26(1).

Felner, Julie. "Playing Hardball." *Ms.,* June/July 1999.

Freedman, Stephen. "The Baseball Fad in Chicago, 1865–1870." *Journal of Sport History,* Summer, 1978, v. 5, n. 2.

Gummer, Scott. "Ila Borders: Pitcher, Southern California College." *Sports Illustrated for Kids,* August 1994 v. 6, n. 8, p. 50(1).

Karlen, Neal. "Ila Borders: A Pitcher Who's in a League of Her Own." *The New York Times,* 6 September 1998.

Lewis, Pamela. "There's Little Rest for L.B.'s Lisa Fernandez." *Long Beach Press/Telegram,* 16 August 1996.

McClatchy, Reid. "First woman to pitch collegiately gets a place in the Hall of Fame." Knight-Ridder/Tribune News Service, 31 January 1995.

Murphy, Austin. "Dot Richardson." *Sports Illustrated,* 18 July 1994, v. 81, n. 3.

Plummer, William. "Double play: on the diamond or in the OR." *People Weekly,* 24 June 1996, v. 45, n. 25.

Polzin, Jim. "Borders gets new life in Madison." *The Capital Times,* 14 June 1999.

Rushin, Steve. "Playing with heart." *Sports Illustrated,* 29 July 1996, v. 85, n. 5, p. 54(4).

Smith, Gene. "The Girls of Summer." *American Heritage,* July-August 1994, v. 45, n. 4, p. 110(2).

Sullivan, Dean. "Replacement players, circa 1883." *Harper's Magazine,* April 1995, v. 290, n. 1739.

Thomas, Robert. "Toni Stone, 75, First Woman to Play Big-League Baseball." *The New York Times,* 10 November 1996.

Wallace, Mike. "A League of Her Own." *60 Minutes.* CBS Worldwide Inc. Show transcript.

Index